Be a Smart Surfer!

The Internet and You

By Noah Hayden

Celebration Press
Pearson Learning Group

CONTENTS

The Internet and You

Chances are that you already know a lot about the **Internet**. You probably send **e-mail** and chat with family and friends. You may play games or listen to music online. Maybe you've used the Internet to research reports for school.

The Internet began in the late 1960s as a small network of computers at universities and U.S. government offices. The network grew steadily, and other countries joined. In the 1980s it became known as the Internet.

The World Wide Web, developed by a British scientist, joined the Internet in 1991. The Web has pictures, sounds, and videos, not just text as the rest of the Internet has. For this reason, it has made the Internet very popular.

Many families enjoy exploring on the Internet together.

The Internet has evolved into a worldwide network serving millions. All you need to connect to this network is a computer with a **modem**, a telephone line, and an Internet service provider.

Today people use the Internet to find all kinds of information, to communicate with other people, and to buy and sell products and services. Students take classes online. Co-workers send reports back and forth. Job hunters look for new positions and distribute their **résumés**. Families share their favorite photos. People read articles in newspapers from many countries, and writers publish books online. On the Internet you can shop for almost any item under the sun. You can even e-mail a pen pal halfway around the world!

More and more people are connecting to the Internet every day, making it one of today's most powerful communications tools.

Computers provide massive amounts of information.

- In 2000, about 300 million people around the world were using the Internet, including more than 90 million people in the United States!
- Today a large number of children in the United States ages 4 to 18 use the Internet.

The Internet can put an amazing amount of information at your fingertips with a few clicks of the mouse. But there can be a catch.

Before most books, newspapers, and magazines are published, someone has to review them to make sure they are accurate and well written. No one has to review information before it's put on the Internet. Anyone can create a **Web site**. That means you can't always expect the information on every site to be accurate, the way you can with facts in an encyclopedia or a major newspaper.

Another challenge posed by the Internet is the mixing of information, entertainment, and business. Sometimes a site that seems to offer good information is really trying to sell something or is entertaining you.

Surfers on the ocean have to be careful and pay close attention to what's around them. When you "surf" the Internet, you also need to pay careful attention in order to judge whether the information you find is reliable or not.

Finding What You're Looking For

The first step in being a smart surfer is knowing how to find what you're looking for. Don't waste your time reading **Web page** after Web page if the information isn't useful. You can use the Internet to help you find exactly the information you want, and usually quickly.

You're probably familiar with **search engines**. They are tools for finding information on the Web. A search engine does the same job as an index in a book. When you use a search engine, you type in words, called **keywords**, that describe the information you want to find. The search engine gives you a list of Web sites that contain information about your keywords.

There are many different kinds of search engines out there. Some have large **databases**, or collections of information organized so it can be found quickly. Examples are Google (http://google.com/) and WebCrawler (http://webcrawler.com/).

Some search engines let you limit your searches to specific subject areas, such as the sciences or even shopping. Some search engines are just for kids, such as KidsClick! (http://www.kidsclick.org).

To find information, type in your keyword(s) and click on "Search." The search engine will search its database to find Web pages that contain your keyword(s). Then it will list the Web sites that match your topic.

How to Perform a Search

Here are some tips you can follow to make searching the Web easier and more rewarding.

1. Choose your keywords carefully.

A search engine is only as good as the words you use in your search. Try to use precise keywords. Let's say your family is thinking about adopting a greyhound from a shelter. You want to find information about this breed of dog. You should use *greyhound* instead of *dog* as your keyword. The more specific the keyword, the fewer Web pages you'll have to look through to find the information you want.

Search for:	greyhound	Search

This search will locate web pages that contain information on the topic *greyhound*.

2. Use more than one keyword, if needed.

Put the most important words first. If you use more than one keyword, you'll usually get results that are closer to what you're looking for. Let's say you want to find out how much exercise your new greyhound needs. You'll get much better results if you use *greyhound exercise* as your keywords than if you used just *greyhound*.

3. Spell your keywords correctly.

Search engines look for exactly what you type. A misspelled word will not give you the results you want. Consult a dictionary if you are not sure of the correct spelling of a word.

4. Use more than one search engine.

No search engine can look through every single page on the Web, and search engines only update their databases of Web pages every so often. So when you're using a search engine, you're only getting results from the Web sites that particular engine has cataloged. It pays to use more than one engine. Some search engines refer you to another one to help you continue your search.

5. Practice!

Like anything else, the more searches you do, the more skillful your searching will become.

Smart Reading on the Web

When a list of sites appears, often there is a short description of each. Read the descriptions to choose the site that appears most helpful.

What do you do once you go to a Web page? You don't need to read every word on every page you come across, searching for the information you want. That would take up too much time.

Skimming and **scanning** are two important strategies that can help you figure out if a Web page is likely to contain the information you need. They let you find the information you need without having to read an entire Web page word for word.

You don't have to read every word to know what most Web pages are about.

9

Skimming involves looking over a Web page quickly to get a general idea of the information it contains. Start by looking for any titles or headings. These will give you an idea of the main topics on the page. Then look at the pictures, diagrams, and charts. Read the captions. These will also help you see what part of the topic the page covers and in how much detail.

Scanning means looking for keywords and specific phrases to find the information you need. Look for important words and phrases in bold or italic type. Look for numbered lists. You can also read the first and last sentence of each paragraph to get an idea of the information each one contains.

If you come across a Web page that has a lot of text, you can use your **Web browser** to help you scan for the information you need. A browser is the program that helps you move around and look for information on the Web. Most Web browsers have a "Find" feature that lets you type in keywords. The browser will then search the Web page for the words you entered. "Find" is a great tool that can save you time on the Internet. If you have trouble, try clicking on "Help" on your tool bar to learn how to use your "Find" feature.

Don't Trust Everything You See!

Now you know some ways to search for information on the Internet and ways to save time by skimming and scanning Web pages. What do you do once you find a Web page that contains the information you're looking for? You need to determine if you can trust the information.

Remember that anyone can create a Web site and put whatever they want on it. Most people don't list their qualifications, so it's sometimes hard to tell if Web page authors know what they're talking about.

The purpose of a Web page is an important factor, too. Does the author have a "hidden agenda"—a hidden plan? For example, is the author selling a product or promoting a cause or a candidate?

Many young people use the Internet at their school or local library.

The purpose of a Web page is not always easy to figure out. There are many different kinds of Web pages. There are personal pages created by people who want to share information about themselves or their favorite topics. There are advocacy, or supporting, pages written by groups that want to teach you about their causes or beliefs and persuade you to accept them. News and informational pages report on various subjects. Finally business and marketing pages often aim to sell you products and services.

Knowing the source of information on a site will help you decide whether the information you find there is likely to be accurate and reliable. Obviously the information in a government report or a news article will be more believable than claims in an ad.

Sometimes information on a Web page seems more reliable than it really is. The Web includes thousands and thousands of pages that look as if they are providing information about a topic. However, some of these pages have been created by businesses that want to sell you something. So the information on these pages isn't always as straightforward or truthful as it seems. There are some ways, though, to help you "test" the reliability and accuracy of the information you come across.

Domain Names

First of all, you should know what kind of Web page you are visiting. The **domain name**—the three-letter part of the Web address after the "dot"— tells the type of Web site. Examples of domain names are listed below.

.com   commercial (business)
.edu   educational institution
.gov   government agency
.mil   military agency
.net   network (private Internet service provider)
.org   nonprofit organization

Commercial and network sites often contain ads, which may affect their content. (If advertisers don't like the content, they won't place an ad on that site.) Government and military sites are good sources for statistics and public and historical information. Educational and organization sites usually have accurate information related to learning.

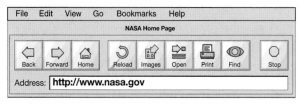

Your Web browser shows the address of the Web page you are visiting.

13

How to Evaluate Information

The following checklist can help you evaluate Web-site information.

1. Accuracy: Is It True?

√ Is the information correct? Are sources given? Remember that a fact can be proven true, but opinions cannot.

√ Are there any spelling mistakes or grammatical errors? These kinds of mistakes sometimes can indicate that the information was not put together carefully or reviewed by a knowledgeable editor.

√ Is the page well designed? Is it neat? A sloppy page should make you question the accuracy of its information. However, don't be deceived by looks! A slick, beautiful page is not always correct.

2. Authority: Who Published the Information?

√ What is the domain? Personal pages may be less reliable than pages backed by an organization.

√ What person or organization posted the information on the Web site? Is he, she, or it qualified to provide information about this topic?

√ Is there a way to contact the author or publisher by e-mail or phone to check facts?

3. Objectivity: Is It Fair?

√ What is the purpose of the Web page? Is it intended to persuade you to believe or do something? Is the information provided by a business that wants to sell you something?

√ Does the Web site provide a balanced view on the particular topic, or does it give only one side?

4. Currency: Is It Out of Date?

√ When was the Web page created?

√ When was the page last updated?

√ Does the Web site provide these dates? If you are looking for information about a topic that changes frequently—the latest developments on the International Space Station, for example—you need an up-to-date site.

5. Coverage: How Detailed Is the Information?

√ Does the Web page go into enough detail on the topic and cover all parts of the topic?

√ Are there links to other resources? Are these links available or no longer working?

You may not be able to find answers to all these questions for every Web page you visit. However, it's important for you to keep these questions in mind as you surf the Internet. They will help you determine whether you can trust the information you find.

Evaluation in Action

Now it's time for you to put what you have learned into practice. Look at the Web page on page 17. Think about the strategies you learned to help you evaluate information on Web sites.

What is the purpose of this Web page? It looks as if the author is trying to convince readers that the historic moon walk in 1969 didn't happen. It doesn't appear to be a joke, so you should assume that the author wants you to believe his argument.

He provides two sources to back up his claims. However, very little information from these sources is included, other than the titles of the books and the authors' names. Also, did you notice that both sources are self-published? Perhaps publishing companies didn't want to print this material. Maybe the information isn't as trustworthy as it might seem. There are also spelling and punctuation mistakes. These errors make the information seem even less reliable.

The domain of this Web page is a commercial site, and the author's name is listed at the bottom of the screen. Yet his training in the subject is not listed. There is no way to contact him. This doesn't help make the information more believable.

The Moon Walk Hoax

Back   Forward   Home   Reload   Images   Open   Print   Find   Stop

Address: **http://www.homepage.com/whitehall/moon.html**

The Moon Walk Hoax

On July 20, 1969 two American astronauts, Neil Armstrong and Edwin "Buzz" Aldrin walked on the Moon. Or so our goverment would haveus believe.

While this event was being broadcast on TV, many Americans watched and didn't believe what was happening. Some of these people went on to research this supposed moon landing.

Was this photo really taken in Nevada?

They discovered that the goverment made up the entire thing.

In his self-published book *NASA Mooned America*, Ralph Rene details his findings that the Moon walk was faked by NASA.

Another writer, Bill Kaysing also had a self-published book that outlines his theory that the Moon walk never happened.

Most of these people believe that NASA filmed the astronauts walking on a soundstage in Nevada. They used sand from the desert to simulate the surface of the Moon. NASA did this because the agncy claimed that it would put a man on the Moon by the end of the 1960s. After many technical porblems and mistakes, NASA realized that it would not happen. So they were forced to make the entire thing up.

| How NASA Did It | Why NASA Lied | Faking the Photographs of the Moon Walk | Other Moon Hoax pages |

Created by: James Whitehall
Date created: March 20, 1998
Last updated: January 4, 2002

The argument presented in the article is very one-sided. The author gives only evidence that the walk on the moon did not really happen. He does not offer a fair or objective view. Clearly the author wants to persuade you to believe that the moon walk was a hoax.

What do you think the author's motive is? Why would someone want you to believe that the United States government lied about an event for which there seems to be so much reliable evidence?

The dates the page was created and updated are listed. However, there are too many other problems with this Web page for that information to carry much weight. Just because a Web site is updated frequently doesn't mean you should accept its content without evaluating it first.

Check to determine whether the subject is covered adequately. The information on this page doesn't give many specific details. There are links to more information. However, you'd have to evaluate this other information before making up your mind about its reliability.

So is the information on this Web page likely to be reliable? The answer is no. There are too many problems with the Web site for it to be considered reliable.

Here's another chance for you to sharpen your evaluation skills. Imagine that you want to buy a new video game for your computer. You want something fast-paced and challenging—something that's a lot of fun and really gives you your money's worth.

You come across this Web page that offers a review of a new video game. Read the information on the Web page below. Then decide if you would be willing to buy this game based just on the information given here.

File   Edit   View   Go   Bookmarks   Help

Funhouse!

Back   Forward   Home   Reload   Images   Open   Print   Find   Stop

Address: http://www.compfun.com/funhouse.html

Funhouse!

It's here! The greatest new video game for your computer! You won't believe the incredible graphics and the nonstop action! This one will really test your skills. You'll be breathless for days!

Here's what one reviewer said:
"Funhouse, brought to you by Compfun, combines awesome animation with a challenging objective. It will keep you playing for hours! Your friends won't want to leave your house once they've played Funhouse!"

Requirements:
PC or Mac with minimum 64 MB RAM
CD-ROM drive
3 MB Hard disk space

Order Yours Today!

Copyright 2001 Compfun, Inc.
Date created: April 12, 2001

Evaluating a Review for a Video Game You might be tempted to buy the video game based on how great the game sounds in the review. However, think carefully about this information first.

Did you notice that the company that created and markets the game is the sponsor of this Web page? Look at the address for the Web site. It's a commercial, or business, site created by Compfun. This means that the review of the game could be very biased, that is, favoring just one side.

The review itself gives very little information about the video game. There is no information telling how it works. The language is emotionally charged, using words like *incredible* and *awesome*. The review also suggests that your friends will want to spend more time with you if you have the game. The writer is appealing to your emotions to persuade you to buy the game. Also notice that the Web page doesn't provide any information about who wrote this review. Why should you believe the claims of an unknown reviewer?

In addition, there's not one single image from the game shown in the review. Don't you want to see what the game looks like before deciding to buy it? You'd be taking a big chance if you spent money on the game based on this review alone.

Here is another example. Suppose that you are planning to write a report on the childrens' book illustrator David Diaz. After doing a search, you find this Web page. Would it be reasonable for you to use the information found on this page in your report?

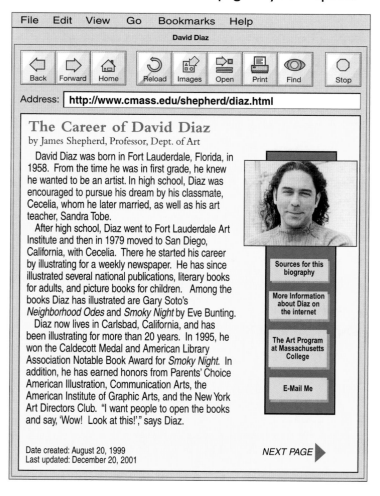

File   Edit   View   Go   Bookmarks   Help

David Diaz

Back   Forward   Home   Reload   Images   Open   Print   Find   Stop

Address: http://www.cmass.edu/shepherd/diaz.html

The Career of David Diaz
by James Shepherd, Professor, Dept. of Art

David Diaz was born in Fort Lauderdale, Florida, in 1958. From the time he was in first grade, he knew he wanted to be an artist. In high school, Diaz was encouraged to pursue his dream by his classmate, Cecelia, whom he later married, as well as his art teacher, Sandra Tobe.

After high school, Diaz went to Fort Lauderdale Art Institute and then in 1979 moved to San Diego, California, with Cecelia. There he started his career by illustrating for a weekly newspaper. He has since illustrated several national publications, literary books for adults, and picture books for children. Among the books Diaz has illustrated are Gary Soto's *Neighborhood Odes* and *Smoky Night* by Eve Bunting.

Diaz now lives in Carlsbad, California, and has been illustrating for more than 20 years. In 1995, he won the Caldecott Medal and American Library Association Notable Book Award for *Smoky Night*. In addition, he has earned honors from Parents' Choice American Illustration, Communication Arts, the American Institute of Graphic Arts, and the New York Art Directors Club. "I want people to open the books and say, 'Wow! Look at this!'," says Diaz.

Sources for this biography

More Information about Diaz on the internet

The Art Program at Massachusetts College

E-Mail Me

Date created: August 20, 1999
Last updated: December 20, 2001

NEXT PAGE ▶

Evaluating a Biography   Look carefully at "The Career of David Diaz" Web page shown on page 21. First, the domain name shows that this site is connected with an educational institution. The author of the information is listed, and you can contact him by e-mail. The author is a professor of art at a college. He definitely seems qualified to write about a children's book illustrator.

The page provides links to the sources he used to write the biography. It would be easy for you to check the accuracy of the information. There are also links to other sites about David Diaz, which might be very useful in providing information for your report.

The Web page seems to be the beginning of an article that goes into depth about the career of David Diaz. You can click on "NEXT PAGE" for more facts about Diaz. The information doesn't seem biased in any way, which also makes this page more likely to be reliable. Notice that the creation date of the page is listed, as is the date the page was updated.

All in all, this Web page seems to provide reliable information about the career of David Diaz.

Be a Smart Surfer!

Don't be afraid to surf the Internet. You shouldn't think that most sites are unreliable or that everyone is out to take advantage of you simply because some people are not honest. You just need to be smart and to think carefully about the information you discover while surfing.

Obviously some sites are more trustworthy than others. Check them out. Many sites offer useful information or entertainment. The Internet can be one of the most useful tools you have for learning, communicating, or just having fun as long as you know how to use it wisely!

Young people surf the net to learn, to keep in touch, and just to have fun.

Tips for Online Safety

Remember that the Internet can put you in touch with many different people and ideas. Keep these tips in mind when using the Internet.

Never give out personal information, such as your last name, address, or telephone number, or send a photo of yourself to anyone online without your parents' or guardians' permission.

Never agree to meet a person you've met online unless you have your parents' or guardians' permission. Even then, meet in a public place and have an adult go with you.

Never share your password for e-mail and other Internet applications except with your parents or guardians.

Tell your parents or teacher if you come across any information that is scary or makes you feel uncomfortable. This includes messages you may receive from people online.

Sit down with your parents to work out a list of rules for going online. Agree to the amount of time you can spend online each day, as well as sites that are acceptable for you to visit.